.tiny book of.
PARTY
RECIPES

tiny book of.
PARTY
RECIPES

FOR SPECIAL OCCASIONS

Small Pleasures™
· SERIES ·

hm | books

Small Pleasures
· SERIES ·
hm|books

PRESIDENT/CCO *Brian Hart Hoffman*
VICE PRESIDENT/EDITORIAL *Cindy Smith Cooper*
GROUP CREATIVE DIRECTOR *Deanna Rippy Gardner*
ART DIRECTOR *Cailyn Haynes*

EDITORIAL
RECIPE EDITOR *Fran Jensen*
COPY EDITOR *Emma Pitts*
CREATIVE DIRECTOR/PHOTOGRAPHY *Mac Jamieson*
SENIOR PHOTOGRAPHERS *John O'Hagan, Marcy Black Simpson*
PHOTOGRAPHERS *Jim Bathie, William Dickey, Stephanie Welbourne Steele*
ASSISTANT PHOTOGRAPHER *Caroline Smith*
SENIOR DIGITAL IMAGING SPECIALIST *Delisa McDaniel*
DIGITAL IMAGING SPECIALIST *Clark Densmore*
STYLISTS *Sidney Bragiel, Lucy Herndon, Yukie McLean, Tracey Runnion*
FOOD STYLISTS AND RECIPE DEVELOPERS *Melissa Gray, Elizabeth Ivey, Kathleen Kanen, Janet Lambert, Nancy McColl, Vanessa Rocchio, Emily Turner*
TEST KITCHEN ASSISTANT *Anita Simpson Spain*

hm
hoffmanmedia

CHAIRMAN OF THE BOARD/CEO *Phyllis Hoffman DePiano*
PRESIDENT/COO *Eric W. Hoffman*
PRESIDENT/CCO *Brian Hart Hoffman*
EXECUTIVE VICE PRESIDENT/CFO *Mary P. Cummings*
EXECUTIVE VICE PRESIDENT/O&M *Greg Baugh*
VICE PRESIDENT/DIGITAL MEDIA *Jon Adamson*
VICE PRESIDENT/EDITORIAL *Cindy Smith Cooper*
VICE PRESIDENT/IMS *Ray Reed*
VICE PRESIDENT/ADMINISTRATION *Lynn Lee Terry*

Hoffman Media
1900 International Park Drive, Suite 50
Birmingham, Alabama 35243
www.hoffmanmedia.com
ISBN # 978-1-940772-39-4
Printed in China

ON THE COVER:
(Front) Chocolate Tartlets, page 88.
(Back) Grapefruit and Basil Royale, page 119.

.contents.

.introduction.

Gathering socially for conversation, delicious food, and beverages has been around for as long as anyone can remember.

WE USUALLY ASSOCIATE A PARTY or get-together with a commemorative event like a birthday, holiday, or other special occasion. People look forward to sharing time together and plenty of food, which is always key to a successful event. In this book, you will be able to create your own fun party menu and make it as simple or with as many courses as you like, depending on time and your desire to do so. Start by determining the number of guests, and then decide if you plan to have small bite-size snacks and appetizers, or small plate meals. If you plan a seated meal, the salads, sides, and entrées would be a nice section to consult for menu planning. Sweet endings are a must, and this selection of desserts can be the crowning touch for your party. Beverages and cocktails whet the whistle too, and provide the ribbon that keeps the party going. Don't forget music, which lightens the moods of visitors during the party. Make sure to complement flavors—strawberry cupcakes might be served with a Champagne cocktail, or beverages can even *be* the dessert! Bringing culinary flavors, people, and good times together always makes for plenty of wonderful memories.

— Cindy

.inspirations.

"Blooms at the door welcome guests and can be snipped from the seasonal garden. Greenery works well too, making a fresh 'hello and welcome'."

PREPARE FOR GUESTS during the calendar year by making plans to celebrate with joyous gatherings, designed to delight. Entertaining, whether in your home or a destination, can be a little more festive with flowers and candlelight. Using wreaths, vases, and single blooms add color to tabletops along with tapers or votive candles. The dinnerware and linens you choose should coordinate with the theme, or you might choose to "mix and match" for a particular color scheme. Greeting guests is the perfect note of hospitality, with beverages to welcome good conversation at the ready and near the front door!

THEMES If you'd like to honor tradition, host a party that captures the vintage atmosphere of parties from the past. Menus can be anything from tea sandwiches and a chilled soup to small sweets. When selecting a theme for an occasion, such as a wedding or anniversary, you might select a seasonal theme or a memorable location that has meaning or significance.

MOOD SETTERS Festive additions to beverages can make a big difference for parties. Try paper umbrellas and fresh fruit garnishes to add appeal. On trays, baskets, and tiered pieces: These are handy items that you can use to serve or display food. Various heights create interest and uses of linens, dinnerware, and serveware make the table more enticing.

PLACECARDS & GLASSWARE TAGS A place marker can be a small take-home gift or handwritten script. The sentiment is the same, and marks the spot! Create tags of any sort for wineglasses with jute and shells as a casual tribute. Other seasons or occasions you might consider small ornaments, bells, or other trinkets.

Appetizers & Snacks

SMALL HANDHELD APPETIZERS THAT
CAN BE SERVED WITH BEVERAGES
FOR PARTIES AND GATHERINGS
AROUND THE BUFFET OR BAR

Camembert with Roasted Grapes

1 (8-ounce) round
    Camembert cheese
2½ cups red seedless
    grapes
2 tablespoons extra-
    virgin olive oil
½ teaspoon salt
½ teaspoon ground
    black pepper
Flatbread crackers,
    to serve

Let Camembert stand at room temperature for
30 minutes.

Preheat oven to 400°. Line a rimmed baking sheet
with foil. Spread grapes in an even layer on prepared
pan. Drizzle with oil, and sprinkle with salt and
pepper, stirring to coat.

Bake until grapes begin to burst but not burn,
20 to 25 minutes. Let rest for at least 5 minutes
(grapes will be very hot inside).

Place cheese on a serving dish. Spoon grapes
over cheese. Let rest for 5 minutes before serving.
Serve with flatbread crackers.

Pimiento Cheese Sandwiches

In a medium bowl, stir together cheese, cream cheese, mayonnaise, pimientos, and red pepper until well combined. Divide pimiento cheese mixture among half of bread slices. Top with remaining bread slices. Cut crusts from bread, and discard. Cut sandwiches diagonally into 4 triangles, and serve.

MAKES 12 SERVINGS

**1 cup shredded sharp
   Cheddar cheese**
**2 ounces cream cheese,
   softened**
½ cup mayonnaise
**1 (4-ounce) jar chopped
   pimientos, drained**
**¼ teaspoon ground
   red pepper**
12 slices thin white bread

Cucumber Tea Sandwiches

In the work bowl of a food processor, place cream cheese, dill, and salt; pulse until well combined. Spread mayonnaise onto half of bread slices. Spread cream cheese mixture over remaining bread slices, and top with cucumber and prepared mayonnaise bread slices. Cut crusts from bread, and discard. Cut sandwiches diagonally into 4 triangles, and serve.

MAKES 12 SERVINGS

**3 ounces cream cheese,
   softened**
**2 tablespoons chopped
   fresh dill**
½ teaspoon kosher salt
¼ cup mayonnaise
**12 slices thin whole-wheat
   bread**
**1 medium cucumber, finely
   sliced**

Stovetop Cauliflower Mac and Cheese

3 cups whole milk, divided
2 tablespoons all-purpose
flour
1 ½ cups shredded white
Cheddar cheese
1 ½ cups shredded white
American cheese
1 teaspoon dry mustard
¼ teaspoon kosher salt
¼ teaspoon ground black
pepper
2 (12-ounce) bags steam-in-
bag cauliflower
1 (16-ounce) package medium
pasta shells, cooked
according to package
directions

In a large saucepan, bring 2¾ cups milk to a boil over medium-high heat.

In a small bowl, whisk together flour and remaining ¼ cup milk until smooth; gradually whisk into saucepan until milk thickens, about 2 minutes. Reduce heat to medium-low; add cheeses, mustard, salt, and pepper, whisking until smooth.

Cook cauliflower in microwave according to package directions. Add cauliflower and cooked pasta to cheese mixture, stirring to combine. Serve immediately.

SHRIMP BRUSCHETTA

Shrimp Bruschetta

In a medium bowl, combine tomatoes, 2 tablespoons oil, basil, capers, lemon juice, balsamic vinegar, garlic, salt, and pepper.

Cover and set aside. In another medium bowl, combine shrimp, Italian seasoning, and garlic salt; toss gently to coat shrimp.

In a large skillet, heat remaining 2 tablespoons oil over medium-high heat. Add shrimp; cook until pink and firm, 1 to 2 minutes per side.

Spoon about 1 tablespoon tomato mixture on top of each toasted French bread round. Place shrimp on top of tomato mixture.

MAKES 30

2 cups seeded and chopped tomatoes
4 tablespoons olive oil, divided
2 tablespoons chopped fresh basil
1 tablespoon chopped capers
1 tablespoon fresh lemon juice
1 tablespoon balsamic vinegar
2 teaspoons minced garlic
½ teaspoon salt
¼ teaspoon ground black pepper
30 jumbo fresh shrimp, peeled and deveined
2 teaspoons Italian seasoning
½ teaspoon garlic salt
30 toasted French bread rounds

Shrimp and Cucumber Bites

In a medium bowl, combine shrimp, cucumber, Dijon Vinaigrette, salt, and pepper, tossing gently to coat. Cover and refrigerate for at least 2 hours. Drain, discarding marinade.

Layer 1 cucumber slice and 1 shrimp on cut side of each tomato half. Garnish with fresh parsley, if desired. Serve immediately.

MAKES 24

24 medium fresh shrimp, peeled, deveined, and cooked
24 (¼-inch-thick) slices English cucumber
½ cup Dijon Vinaigrette (recipe on page 53)
½ teaspoon kosher salt
¼ teaspoon ground black pepper
12 Campari tomatoes, halved
Garnish: fresh parsley

Tarragon Chicken Salad with Grapes and Pecans

MAKES ABOUT 4 CUPS

½ cup mayonnaise
½ cup sour cream
1 tablespoon fresh
  lemon juice
1 tablespoon Dijon
  mustard
1 teaspoon kosher salt
3 cups finely chopped
  cooked chicken*
2 stalks celery, diced
1 cup toasted pecans,
  chopped
1 cup red grapes,
  quartered
¼ cup fresh tarragon,
  chopped
Assorted crackers,
  to serve

*Rotisserie chicken may be used.

In a medium bowl, combine mayonnaise, sour cream, lemon juice, mustard, and salt; whisk until well combined.

In another medium bowl, toss together chicken, celery, pecans, grapes, and tarragon. Add mayonnaise mixture, stirring to combine. Serve with assorted crackers.

— Entertaining TIP —

For a simple appetizer, a hollowed-out yellow pepper holds creamy dip to spread on crackers.

Breaded Chicken Satay

In a medium bowl, whisk together flour, salt, and pepper.

In another medium bowl, whisk together milk and egg until combined.

Place bread crumbs in a third medium bowl. Dredge chicken in flour mixture; dip in milk mixture, and dredge in bread crumbs.

In a large skillet, pour oil to a depth of ½ inch, and heat over medium heat until a deep-fry thermometer registers 350°. Fry chicken in batches until golden brown, 3 to 4 minutes per side. Thread 2 pieces of chicken onto each skewer. Serve immediately with Ranch Dip.

RANCH DIP In a medium bowl, stir together all ingredients until combined.

MAKES ABOUT 24

2 cups all-purpose flour
1 teaspoon kosher salt
**½ teaspoon ground
    black pepper**
1 cup whole milk
1 large egg, lightly beaten
**2 cups panko (Japanese
    bread crumbs)**
**2 pounds boneless skinless
    chicken breasts, cut into
    1-inch pieces**
Vegetable oil, for frying
24 (5-inch) wooden skewers
Ranch Dip (recipe follows)

RANCH DIP
MAKES ABOUT 1 CUP

½ cup sour cream
⅓ cup whole buttermilk
**1 tablespoon chopped
    fresh tarragon**
**1 tablespoon chopped
    fresh dill**
**1 tablespoon chopped
    fresh parsley**
½ teaspoon lemon zest
2 teaspoons fresh lemon juice
¼ teaspoon kosher salt
**¼ teaspoon ground black
    pepper**

Barbecue Chicken Dip

**6 cups chopped
cooked chicken**
**1 (15.5-ounce) can
black beans, rinsed
and drained**
**1 (11-ounce) can whole
kernel yellow corn
with red and green
bell peppers,***
drained
**2½ cups shredded
Monterey Jack
cheese, divided**
**2½ cups shredded sharp
Cheddar cheese,
divided**
**½ cup finely chopped
green onion**
**1½ cups hickory-
flavored barbecue
sauce**
1 cup sour cream
¾ teaspoon salt
**¾ teaspoon ground
red pepper**
**½ teaspoon ground
black pepper**
Tortilla chips, to serve

**We used Green Giant
Mexicorn.*

Preheat oven to 350°.

In a large bowl, combine chicken, beans, corn, 2 cups Monterey Jack, 2 cups Cheddar, and green onion.

In another large bowl, combine barbecue sauce, sour cream, salt, red pepper, and black pepper, stirring to mix well. Combine chicken mixture and barbecue sauce mixture, stirring to mix well.

Spoon mixture into a 2-quart baking dish. Sprinkle with remaining ½ cup Monterey Jack and remaining ½ cup Cheddar.

Bake until hot and bubbly, about 30 minutes. Serve with tortilla chips.

Green Chile-Chicken Mini Pizzas

Preheat oven to 350°.

On a large rimmed baking sheet, arrange pita rounds in an even layer. In a medium bowl, stir together chicken and chiles; spoon on top of pitas. Sprinkle with cheese.

Bake until cheese is melted, about 5 minutes. Garnish with cilantro, if desired.

MAKES 24

24 mini pita rounds*
1½ cups chopped
cooked chicken
1 (4-ounce) can chopped
green chiles, drained
⅔ cup shredded
Monterey Jack
cheese
Garnish: chopped
fresh cilantro

*We used Joseph's Mini Pita Rounds.

Escape the chilly winter weather and roll the dice! A game night is the perfect way to bring friends and family together for a laid-back evening that will lead to lots of fun—and a little healthy competition.

Meatballs with Honey-Orange Glaze

MAKES 36

2 pounds ground pork
1 cup fresh bread crumbs
1 large egg
1 teaspoon kosher salt
½ teaspoon onion powder
¼ teaspoon ground black
pepper
2 tablespoons vegetable oil
½ cup honey
⅓ cup orange juice
Garnish: chopped green
onion

Preheat oven to 400°.

In a large bowl, combine pork, bread crumbs, egg, salt, onion powder, and pepper. Stir gently, and roll into 36 balls.

In a large skillet, heat oil over medium-high heat. Add half of meatballs, and cook, turning occasionally, until browned, about 3 minutes.

Remove using a slotted spoon, and place on a rimmed baking sheet. Repeat procedure with remaining meatballs.

Bake until done, about 8 minutes.

Add honey and orange juice to skillet; cook over medium-high heat, stirring frequently, until thickened, about 2 minutes. Remove from heat.

Add meatballs; stir until coated in glaze. Garnish with green onion, if desired.

Recipe TIP

Meatballs can be made a day ahead.
Reheat in a skillet over medium heat.

Steak Fajita Egg Rolls

In a large skillet, heat oil over medium-high heat. Add steak, bell pepper, onion, salt, and pepper; cook, stirring occasionally, until steak is browned and vegetables are tender, 8 to 10 minutes.

Stir in corn, beans, cheese, chiles, salt, and cumin. Spoon mixture into a medium bowl; cover and refrigerate for 1 hour.

Spoon about ¼ cup mixture into center of each wonton wrapper. Fold top corner of each wrapper over filling, tucking tip of corner under filling, and fold left and right corners over filling. Lightly brush remaining corner with water; tightly roll filled end toward remaining corner, and gently press to seal.

In a large Dutch oven, pour oil to a depth of 4 inches, and heat over medium heat until a deep-fry thermometer registers 350°. Fry egg rolls in batches until golden brown, 5 to 6 minutes.

Let drain on paper towels. Serve with Salsa Verde Sauce.

SALSA VERDE SAUCE In a small bowl, stir together salsa verde and sour cream. Cover and refrigerate for up to 5 days.

MAKES 24

1 tablespoon olive oil
1½ pounds flank steak, cut into ¼-inch pieces
1 red bell pepper, chopped
½ cup chopped onion
¾ teaspoon salt
½ teaspoon ground black pepper
1 (15-ounce) can corn, drained
1 (15-ounce) can black beans, rinsed and drained
1 (8-ounce) package shredded Monterey Jack cheese with peppers
1 (4-ounce) can diced green chiles, drained
1 teaspoon garlic salt
1 teaspoon ground cumin
24 wonton wrappers
Vegetable oil, for frying
Salsa Verde Sauce (recipe follows)

SALSA VERDE SAUCE
1 (16-ounce) jar salsa verde
1 cup sour cream

Deviled Eggs

12 large eggs
6 tablespoons mayonnaise
¼ cup sweet pickle relish
1 tablespoon whole-grain
 Dijon mustard
1½ teaspoons yellow
 mustard
1 teaspoon Dijon mustard
2 teaspoons dill pickle juice
¼ teaspoon celery seed
¼ teaspoon ground black
 pepper
Garnish: paprika

Place eggs in a large saucepan with cold water to cover. Bring to a boil over high heat. Reduce heat to medium; simmer for 10 minutes. Remove from heat; drain eggs, and rinse with cold water.

Peel eggs, discarding shells. Cut eggs in half lengthwise. Remove yolks, and place in a small bowl.

Mash yolks with a fork until crumbly. Add mayonnaise, pickle relish, mustards, dill pickle juice, celery seed, and pepper, stirring until well combined.

Spoon egg yolk mixture into egg whites. Garnish with paprika, if desired.

Bacon-Topped Deviled Eggs

Makes 36

18 large eggs
½ cup mayonnaise
6 tablespoons sweet pickle
 relish
1 tablespoon dill pickle juice
2 teaspoons yellow mustard
½ teaspoon ground black
 pepper
Garnish: cooked crumbled
 bacon

Place eggs in a large saucepan with cold water to cover; cook over high heat until water begins to boil. Reduce heat to medium; simmer for 10 minutes. Remove from heat; drain eggs, and rinse with cold water.

Peel eggs, discarding shells. Cut eggs in half lengthwise. Remove yolks, and place in a small bowl. Mash yolks with a fork until crumbly. Add mayonnaise, sweet pickle relish, dill pickle juice, mustard, and pepper, stirring until well combined. Spoon egg yolk mixture into egg whites. Garnish with bacon, if desired.

DEVILED EGGS

Sun-Dried Tomato Dip

Preheat oven to 375°. Spray a 1½-quart baking dish with cooking spray.

In the work bowl of a food processor, pulse tomatoes until coarsely chopped. Add cream cheese, sour cream, and mayonnaise; pulse until combined.

Stir in 1 cup cheese. Spoon into prepared pan. Sprinkle with bread crumbs and remaining ½ cup cheese.

Bake until heated through, about 30 minutes.

Serve with crackers, bell pepper strips, celery strips, and carrot strips.

MAKES ABOUT 4 CUPS

2 (7.5-ounce) jars oil-packed sun-dried tomatoes, drained
2 (8-ounce) packages cream cheese, softened
1 cup sour cream
½ cup mayonnaise
1½ cups Italian cheese blend, divided
1 tablespoon panko (Japanese bread crumbs)
Crackers, bell pepper strips, celery strips, and carrot strips, to serve

Sweet and Spicy Snack Mix

6 cups thin pretzel sticks
1 cup roasted salted peanuts
¼ cup melted butter
1 tablespoon sugar
½ teaspoon smoked paprika
¼ teaspoon ground red pepper
1 (2.3-ounce) package plain salted popcorn, popped according to package directions

Preheat oven to 350°.

In a large bowl, combine pretzels, peanuts, melted butter, sugar, paprika, and red pepper; toss well. Transfer to a large rimmed baking sheet.

Bake until heated through, about 10 minutes, stirring occasionally. Let cool completely on a wire rack.

Transfer mixture to a large bowl, and add popcorn, tossing gently to combine.

Bowls shaped like timeless gaming accessories such as a spade, a heart or club, are fun to have on hand for serving.

Recipe TIP

Recipe can be made a
day ahead. Store in an
airtight container.

ROSEMARY-ROASTED PECANS

Rosemary-Roasted Cashews

Preheat oven to 350°. Line a large rimmed baking sheet with parchment paper. Spread cashews in an even layer on prepared pan.

Bake until golden brown, 8 to 10 minutes, stirring halfway through.

In a large bowl, combine butter, rosemary, and salt. Add hot cashews, stirring to coat well. Store in an airtight container for up to 1 month.

MAKES 5 CUPS

5 cups raw whole cashews
3 tablespoons
**   unsalted butter**
2 tablespoons chopped
**   fresh rosemary leaves**
1 tablespoon sea salt

Rosemary-Roasted Pecans

Preheat oven to 250°.

On a rimmed baking sheet, arrange pecans in a single layer, and sprinkle with butter. Place in oven until butter melts, about 10 minutes.

Stir pecans to coat with melted butter. Add honey, rosemary, salt, and red pepper, tossing to coat.

Bake until golden brown, about 50 minutes, stirring often to prevent burning.

MAKES 2 CUPS

1 pound pecan halves
2 tablespoons unsalted
**   butter, cubed**
2 tablespoons honey
1 tablespoon chopped
**   fresh rosemary**
1 teaspoon salt
½ teaspoon ground
**   red pepper**

Salads, Sides & Entrées

THESE RECIPES CAN BE ENJOYED
SERVED FROM THE BUFFET,
OR PLATED FOR EACH GUEST.

Fresh Fruit Salad with Lime Simple Syrup

1 cup sugar
2 tablespoons lime zest
½ cup fresh lime juice
½ cup water
6 cups fresh orange
    segments
4 cups fresh strawberries,
    sliced
¼ cup fresh mint, chopped
¼ cup sliced almonds,
    toasted

In a small saucepan, bring sugar, zest, lime juice, and ½ cup water to a boil over medium-high heat. Cook, stirring occasionally, until sugar is dissolved. Remove from heat, and strain through fine-mesh sieve into small bowl. Let cool completely.

In a large serving bowl, combine oranges, strawberries, and mint. Add lime syrup, stirring gently to combine. Cover and refrigerate for at least 1 hour.

Just before serving, sprinkle with almonds.

Recipe TIP

Lime syrup can be made a day ahead. Cover and refrigerate until ready to use.

Winter Salad with Creamy Thyme Dressing

In a large bowl, combine lettuce, endive, radicchio, and cranberries. Divide among 8 salad plates.

Top with pear slices. Drizzle with Creamy Thyme Dressing. Garnish with walnuts, if desired.

CREAMY THYME DRESSING In a medium bowl, whisk together all ingredients until combined. Store in an airtight container in refrigerator for up to 1 week.

MAKES 8 SERVINGS

1 head red leaf lettuce,
    washed, dried, and torn
1 head endive, leaves
    separated
½ head radicchio, thinly
    sliced
1 cup dried cranberries
1 red pear, thinly sliced
1 green pear, thinly sliced
Creamy Thyme Dressing
    (recipe follows)
Garnish: toasted walnuts

CREAMY THYME DRESSING
MAKES ABOUT 2½ CUPS

2 cups mayonnaise
½ cup whole buttermilk
¼ cup white wine vinegar
3 tablespoons chopped
    fresh thyme
1 tablespoon Dijon mustard
½ teaspoon garlic powder
½ teaspoon ground black
    pepper
¼ teaspoon garlic salt

BLT Chicken Salad Stuffed Tomatoes

MAKES ABOUT 30

2 cups chopped cooked chicken
8 slices bacon, cooked and crumbled
3/4 cup mayonnaise
1/3 cup finely chopped celery
2 tablespoons finely chopped green onion
1/2 teaspoon ground black pepper, divided
2 (1-pound) containers small Campari tomatoes (about 30 tomatoes)
1/4 teaspoon salt
Garnish: finely shredded green leaf lettuce, cooked crumbled bacon

In a medium bowl, combine chicken, bacon, mayonnaise, celery, green onion, and 1/4 teaspoon pepper; cover and refrigerate.

Using a serrated knife, cut a thin slice off bottom of tomatoes to create a level base. Cut tops from tomatoes. Using a melon baller, remove pulp, leaving shells intact.

Turn tomatoes upside down on paper towels to drain for 10 minutes. Sprinkle inside of tomato shells with salt and remaining 1/4 teaspoon pepper.

Spoon chicken salad into each tomato shell. Garnish with lettuce and bacon, if desired.

Asparagus Salad with Dijon Vinaigrette

Bring a large pot of water to a boil over high heat; add asparagus. When water returns to a boil, immediately drain, and plunge asparagus into an ice bath to stop the cooking process.

In a large bowl, combine asparagus, fennel, radish, onion, shallot, salt, and pepper. Drizzle with Dijon Vinaigrette, tossing gently to coat. Garnish with dill, mint, and almonds, if desired.

DIJON VINAIGRETTE In a small bowl, combine vinegar and shallot; let stand for 15 minutes.

Add parsley, honey, mustard, salt, and pepper, whisking until combined. Gradually drizzle in oil, whisking until combined.

Cover and refrigerate for at least 2 hours or up to 3 days.

MAKES 6 TO 8 SERVINGS

2 (1-pound) bunches fresh
  asparagus, trimmed
1 fennel bulb, thinly sliced
1 cup sliced radish
½ cup thinly sliced red onion
1 shallot, thinly sliced
½ teaspoon kosher salt
½ teaspoon ground black
  pepper
Dijon Vinaigrette (recipe
  follows)
Garnish: fresh dill, fresh
  mint, shredded toasted
  almonds

DIJON VINAIGRETTE
MAKES 1 CUP

¼ cup Champagne vinegar
2 tablespoons minced
  shallot
2 tablespoons chopped fresh
  parsley
2 tablespoons honey
2 tablespoons Dijon mustard
¼ teaspoon kosher salt
¼ teaspoon ground black
  pepper
¾ cup olive oil

Chicken Taco Salads

1 (6.8-ounce) box
    Spanish rice
2 tablespoons
    vegetable oil
1 (1.25-ounce) package
    taco seasoning mix
2 pounds boneless
    skinless chicken
    breasts
2 (15-ounce) cans
    black beans, rinsed
    and drained
1 (8-ounce) package
    shredded lettuce
1 (16-ounce) container
    sour cream
1 (8-ounce) package
    shredded Cheddar
    cheese
3 plum tomatoes,
    chopped
½ cup chopped green
    onion

Prepare rice according to package directions. Spread hot cooked rice onto a rimmed baking sheet. Cover and refrigerate for at least 2 hours or up to 2 days.

In a large resealable plastic bag, combine oil and seasoning mix. Add chicken; seal bag, and shake to coat.

Spray grill rack with nonflammable cooking spray. Preheat grill to medium-high heat (350° to 400°).

Grill chicken for 6 to 8 minutes per side. Let stand for 20 minutes. Cut into ¼ -inch pieces.

In individual serving dishes, layer rice, chicken, beans, and all remaining ingredients.

Cover and refrigerate for up to 2 days, or serve immediately.

Avocado and Grapefruit Salad

Arrange lettuce leaves on serving plates. Top with grapefruit and avocado.

In a medium bowl, whisk together ¼ cup reserved grapefruit juice, oil, tarragon, salt, and pepper. Drizzle over salad. Serve immediately.

MAKES 8 SERVINGS

2 heads butter lettuce,
   washed and torn
4 grapefruit, peeled and
   sectioned, juice reserved
4 avocados, peeled and
   sliced
¼ cup extra-virgin olive oil
2 tablespoons fresh tarragon
   leaves
½ teaspoon salt
½ teaspoon ground black
   pepper

Entertaining TIP

Accents like soft chambray napkins with a scalloped trim and lattice-looking napkin rings in bright green complement a pink and green color scheme.

Roasted Rainbow Carrot Medley

Makes 6 servings

4 (6-ounce) packages miniature
    rainbow carrots, halved
    lengthwise
4 cloves elephant garlic,
    peeled and halved
3 shallots, quartered
¼ cup olive oil
1 tablespoon kosher salt
2 teaspoons ground
    black pepper
Garnish: fresh thyme sprigs

Preheat oven to 375°. Line a rimmed baking sheet with foil.

Place carrots, garlic, and shallot on prepared pan. Drizzle with oil, and sprinkle with salt and pepper.

Bake until tender, about 25 minutes. Garnish with thyme, if desired.

Elephant garlic, contrary to its name, is not actually a member of the garlic family but is more closely related to the leek. This bulb is milder in flavor than regular garlic but is much larger, often the size of a grapefruit!

Harvest Medley

Preheat oven to 425°. Line a rimmed baking sheet with foil.

In a large bowl, combine garlic, shallots, carrot, apples, radishes, Brussels sprouts, and rosemary sprigs. Add oil and melted butter, and toss to coat. Sprinkle with salt, pepper, and rosemary.

Bake until lightly browned and tender, 25 to 30 minutes. Serve immediately. Garnish with fresh sage, if desired.

MAKES 8 TO 10 SERVINGS

6 cloves garlic
3 shallots, quartered
2 (8-ounce) packages
    miniature rainbow
    carrots, cut in half
2 red apples, quartered
2 green apples, quartered
1 bunch radishes with
    green tops, trimmed
    and cut in half
1 pound Brussels sprouts,
    peeled, trimmed, and
    cut in half
4 sprigs fresh rosemary
¼ cup olive oil
¼ cup butter, melted
2 teaspoons kosher salt
1 teaspoon ground black
    pepper
1 tablespoon chopped
    fresh rosemary
Garnish: fresh sage

Butternut Squash Soup

MAKES ABOUT 3 QUARTS

¼ cup unsalted butter
2 cups diced sweet onion
2 cloves garlic, minced
8 cups (¼-inch-cubed)
  butternut squash
8 cups vegetable stock
2 cups heavy whipping
  cream
¼ cup honey
1 tablespoon kosher salt
2 teaspoons ground
  allspice
1 teaspoon ground
  cinnamon
½ teaspoon ground red
  pepper
¼ teaspoon ground
  nutmeg
2 tablespoons chopped
  fresh sage
Garnish: crème fraîche,
  toasted walnuts, fresh
  sage leaves

In a large stockpot, melt butter over medium-high heat. Add onion and garlic; cook, stirring frequently, until translucent, about 3 minutes. Add squash; cook for 8 minutes, stirring frequently. Add stock, and bring to a boil; reduce heat, and simmer until squash is cooked through, about 15 minutes.

Transfer squash mixture to the container of a blender in batches. Secure lid on blender, and remove center piece of lid to let steam escape; place a clean towel over opening in lid to avoid splatters. Process on high until smooth; return to pot.

Add cream, honey, salt, allspice, cinnamon, red pepper, and nutmeg; bring to a boil over high heat. Reduce to a simmer, and cook for 10 minutes; stir in sage. Serve immediately, or cover and store for up to 3 days. Garnish with crème fraîche, walnuts, and sage, if desired.

Chicken Tortilla Soup

In a Dutch oven, heat 2 tablespoons oil over medium-high heat. Add onion, garlic, shallot, and poblano; cook mixture, stirring often, until tender, about 5 minutes.

Add 1 cup broth to pan; simmer for 5 minutes. Add remaining 4 cups broth, 1 cup water, corn kernels, creamed corn, tomatoes, and chicken to pan. Reduce heat to medium, and simmer for 20 minutes.

Add lime juice, salt, and pepper, stirring to combine. Add avocado and cilantro.

In a cast-iron skillet, heat remaining 1 tablespoon oil over medium-high heat. Add tortilla strips, and cook, stirring often, until crisp, about 5 minutes.

Serve soup with tortilla strips. Garnish with queso fresco, radish, and cilantro, if desired.

MAKES 8 SERVINGS

3 tablespoons vegetable oil, divided
1½ cups chopped yellow onion
4 cloves garlic, minced
1 shallot, finely chopped
1 poblano pepper, stemmed, seeded, and chopped
5 cups chicken broth, divided
1 cup water
2 (11-ounce) cans yellow corn kernels, drained
1 (14.75-ounce) can creamed corn
1 (10-ounce) can diced tomatoes with green chiles*
1 rotisserie chicken, meat pulled from bone
3 tablespoons fresh lime juice
1½ tablespoons kosher salt
½ teaspoon ground black pepper
1 ripe avocado, peeled, cored, and sliced
2 tablespoons coarsely chopped fresh cilantro
6 corn tortillas, cut into ½-inch strips
Garnish: queso fresco, sliced fresh radish, fresh cilantro

*We used Ro-Tel.

Spicy Chipotle Chili

MAKES 8 SERVINGS

2 pounds lean ground
beef
2 tablespoons olive oil
2 cups chopped yellow
onion
1 tablespoon minced
garlic
3 cups water
2 (16-ounce) cans hot
chili beans,
undrained
2 (14.5-ounce) cans
fire-roasted diced
tomatoes
2½ tablespoons chili
powder
2 chipotle peppers in
adobo sauce, minced
2 tablespoons adobo
sauce
1 tablespoon firmly
packed dark brown
sugar
2 teaspoons ground
cumin
1¼ teaspoons salt
1 teaspoon ground
black pepper
½ teaspoon garlic
powder
½ teaspoon dried
oregano

In a Dutch oven, cook beef over medium-high heat until browned, about 8 minutes. Remove meat from pan; drain well.

In same pan, heat oil over medium heat. Add onion and garlic; cook for 5 minutes, stirring frequently.

Add cooked beef, 3 cups water, chili beans, and all remaining ingredients, stirring to combine.

Bring to a boil; reduce heat to medium-low, and cook, covered, for 1 hour, stirring occasionally.

Recipe TIP

Smoked jalapeño peppers, known as chipotle peppers, are responsible for the spice in this dish.

66 *Tiny Book of Party Recipes* | Salads, Sides & Entrées

Stuffed Crêpe Casserole

Preheat oven to 350°. Spray a 13x9-inch baking dish with cooking spray.

In a large skillet, melt butter over medium-high heat. Add onion and garlic; cook, stirring frequently, until tender, about 5 minutes. Add spinach, and cook until wilted. Stir in flour, and cook for 2 minutes, stirring constantly.

Gradually add broth, stirring until smooth. Add half-and-half, 1 cup cheese, salt, and pepper. Cook over medium heat, whisking until cheese is melted and mixture is smooth. Reserve 1 cup cream sauce in a small bowl. Stir chicken into remaining cream mixture in skillet. Let mixture cool completely.

Spoon ½ to ¾ cup chicken mixture into center of each crêpe, and roll up to enclose filling. Place each crêpe, seam side down, in prepared pan. Pour reserved 1 cup cream sauce over crêpes. Sprinkle with remaining ½ cup cheese.

Bake until cheese is lightly browned, 15 to 20 minutes. Garnish with oregano, if desired.

MAKES 10 SERVINGS

⅓ cup butter
1 cup chopped onion
1 tablespoon minced garlic
1 (5-ounce) bag fresh baby spinach
¼ cup all-purpose flour
2 cups chicken broth
½ cup half-and-half
1½ cups grated Asiago cheese, divided
1½ teaspoons kosher salt
1 teaspoon ground black pepper
3 cups shredded rotisserie chicken
1 (5-ounce) package refrigerated prepared crêpes
Garnish: fresh oregano

Caribbean Shrimp Skewers

3 tablespoons olive oil
2 teaspoons paprika
1 teaspoon kosher salt
1 teaspoon ground ancho
  chile pepper
½ teaspoon garlic powder
½ teaspoon ground allspice
1 pound medium fresh shrimp,
  peeled and deveined
  (tails left on)
1 fresh pineapple, peeled,
  cored, and cut into 1-inch
  cubes
1 red onion, cut into 1-inch
  cubes
12 (12-inch) wooden skewers,
  soaked in water for
  30 minutes
Roasted Red Pepper Sauce
  (recipe follows)
Garnish: fresh cilantro leaves

ROASTED RED PEPPER SAUCE
Makes 1½ cups

4 medium red bell peppers,
  halved and seeded
1 tablespoon olive oil
¼ cup Greek yogurt
3 tablespoons heavy
  whipping cream
1 teaspoon kosher salt
1 teaspoon ground ancho
  chile pepper

In a large bowl, whisk together oil, paprika, salt, chile pepper, garlic powder, and allspice. Add shrimp, tossing to coat. Thread shrimp, pineapple, and onion onto skewers.

Spray grill rack with nonflammable cooking spray. Preheat grill to medium-high heat (350° to 400°).

Grill skewers until shrimp are pink and firm, 3 to 5 minutes per side. Serve with Roasted Red Pepper Sauce. Garnish with cilantro, if desired.

ROASTED RED PEPPER SAUCE Preheat oven to 450°. Line a rimmed baking sheet with foil.

Place bell peppers, cut side down, on prepared pan. Drizzle with oil, and cover with foil.

Bake until softened and lightly browned, about 20 minutes. Let stand until cool enough to handle, about 20 minutes. Gently remove outer skin and stems.

In the container of a blender, combine bell pepper, yogurt, and all remaining ingredients; process on high until smooth, about 2 minutes.

Cover and refrigerate for up to 3 days.

Recipe TIP

Serve skewers on a bed of black beans, rice, and avocado for a colorful presentation.

Chicken Pot Pie

Preheat oven to 400°. Spray 8 (8- to 10-ounce) baking dishes with cooking spray.

In a large saucepan, bring potatoes and water to cover to a boil over medium-high heat. Cover and cook for 10 minutes; drain.

In a large Dutch oven, heat oil over medium-high heat. Add carrot, onion, and celery; cook, stirring frequently, until onion is translucent and celery and carrot are slightly softened, about 5 minutes. Stir in butter. Add flour; cook for 2 minutes, stirring constantly. Stir in milk and broth; cook, whisking occasionally, until sauce comes to a boil and thickens, about 8 minutes. Stir in sherry, salt, thyme, garlic powder, and pepper until combined. Stir in chicken, potatoes, and peas. Spoon mixture into prepared pans.

On a lightly floured surface, divide each pastry sheet into 4 squares, and place on top of each baking dish. In a small bowl, whisk together egg and 1 tablespoon water. Using a pastry brush, brush egg mixture on top of pastry squares.

Bake until crust is golden brown and filling is bubbling, 20 to 25 minutes. Serve immediately.

MAKES 8 SERVINGS

1½ pounds new potatoes, quartered
¼ cup canola oil
3 cups shredded carrot
2 cups chopped yellow onion
2 cups chopped celery
6 tablespoons butter
¾ cup all-purpose flour
2¼ cups whole milk
2¼ cups chicken broth
6 tablespoons dry cooking sherry
1 tablespoon kosher salt
1 tablespoon dried thyme
1½ teaspoons garlic powder
¾ teaspoon ground white pepper
6 cups cooked chicken
3 cups frozen peas, thawed
1 (17.3-ounce) package frozen puff pastry, thawed
1 large egg
1 tablespoon water

Recipe TIP

Brushing pastry dough with an "egg wash" helps make the pastry golden brown when baked and serves as an adherent for additional toppings such as nuts, seeds, or sugar crystals. It is also used to seal pastry dough (such as when sealing pie dough to make a fried pie).

Cobb Salad Burgers

MAKES 6 SERVINGS

1 (20-ounce) package
  ground turkey
1 pound ground pork
¼ cup minced celery
2 tablespoons minced
  fresh parsley
1 tablespoon Dijon
  mustard
1 teaspoon salt
1 teaspoon ground
  black pepper
6 hamburger buns,
  halved and toasted
Toppings: blue cheese
  dressing, lettuce
  leaves, sliced
  tomato, dill pickle
  slices, alfalfa
  sprouts, sliced
  avocado, bacon

Spray grill rack with nonflammable cooking spray. Preheat grill to medium-high heat (350° to 400°).

In a large bowl, stir together turkey, pork, celery, parsley, mustard, salt, and pepper. Divide mixture into 6 portions, and shape each into a 5-inch patty.

Grill burgers, covered with grill lid, until a meat thermometer inserted in thickest portion registers 155°, 5 to 6 minutes per side. Let stand for 5 minutes. Serve burgers on toasted buns with desired toppings.

Entertaining TIP

Individual and smaller plates can be
served at the dinner table, indoors or out.

Chipotle Burgers with Peppered Bacon

Spray grill rack with nonflammable cooking spray. Preheat grill to medium-high heat (350° to 400°).

In a large bowl, stir together ground chuck, Worcestershire, horseradish, cumin, pepper, and salt. Divide mixture into 6 portions, and shape each into a 5-inch patty.

Grill burgers, covered with grill lid, until a meat thermometer inserted in thickest portion registers 155°, 5 to 6 minutes per side. Let stand for 5 minutes. Serve burgers on toasted buns with Chipotle Ketchup, Fried Red Onions, and desired toppings.

CHIPOTLE KETCHUP In the container of a blender, process all ingredients until smooth. Cover and refrigerate for up to 5 days.

FRIED RED ONIONS In a large bowl, toss together onions and cornmeal.

In a medium saucepan, pour oil to a depth of 3 inches, and heat over medium heat until a deep-fry thermometer registers 350°. Add onions, in batches, and fry until golden brown, 2 to 3 minutes. Let drain on paper towels.

MAKES 6 SERVINGS

2 pounds ground chuck
2 tablespoons Worcestershire
    sauce
1 tablespoon prepared horseradish
1 teaspoon ground cumin
1 teaspoon ground black pepper
½ teaspoon salt
6 hamburger buns, halved and
    toasted
Chipotle Ketchup (recipe follows)
Fried Red Onions (recipe follows)
Toppings: Monterey Jack cheese,
    lettuce leaves, sliced tomato,
    dill pickle slices, peppered
    bacon

CHIPOTLE KETCHUP
MAKES ABOUT 1¼ CUPS

1 cup ketchup
¼ cup Dijon mustard
2 chipotle peppers in adobo sauce

FRIED RED ONIONS
MAKES ABOUT 6 SERVINGS

2 red onions, very thinly sliced
1 cup cornmeal
Vegetable oil, for frying

Club Sandwich Bites

MAKES ABOUT 36

**2 (1-pound) oval
    sourdough loaves**
½ cup mayonnaise
¼ cup Dijon mustard
**6 slices bacon, cooked
    and crumbled**
½ pound sliced deli turkey
½ pound sliced deli ham
2 medium tomatoes, sliced
**4 large romaine lettuce
    leaves**

Trim about 1 inch from each end of sourdough loaves. Cut each loaf in half horizontally; hollow out excess bread in center of each top, if necessary. Spread cut sides of sourdough with mayonnaise and mustard.

Divide bacon, turkey, ham, tomatoes, and lettuce over bottom half of loaves. Add top half of loaves; gently press.

Using a serrated knife, cut each loaf in half lengthwise, then crosswise at 1-inch intervals. Secure each portion with a wooden pick.

club sandwich

Entertaining TIP

Celebrate a get-together with tagged toothpicks,
either handmade or purchased from a party store.

Reuben Strudels

Preheat oven to 400°. Line 2 baking sheets with parchment paper.

On a lightly floured surface, roll one pastry sheet into a 12x12-inch square. Trim edges of pastry. Spread 2 tablespoons mustard down center of pastry. Layer half of corned beef, half of sauerkraut, and half of cheese down center of pastry on top of mustard.

Cut strips, and braid pastry. Transfer to prepared pan. Repeat procedure with remaining puff pastry, mustard, corned beef, sauerkraut, and cheese.

In a small bowl, whisk together egg and 1 tablespoon water. Lightly brush crusts with egg mixture.

Bake until golden brown, 25 to 30 minutes. Cut into slices to serve.

MAKES 16 SERVINGS

1 (17.3-ounce) package frozen puff pastry, thawed
4 tablespoons whole-grain mustard, divided
1½ pounds sliced corned beef, divided
1 (14.4-ounce) can shredded sauerkraut, well drained and divided
3 cups shredded Swiss cheese, divided
1 large egg
1 tablespoon water

Recipe TIP

Trim both top corners of pastry. Notch opposite short side of pastry. After layering filling as directed in recipe, cut exposed pastry diagonally into strips. Fold top edge of pastry over filling. Braid pastry strips over filling. Tuck ends of pastry strips under at opposite end.

Desserts

A LITTLE SOMETHING SWEET IS
ALWAYS NICE AFTER APPETIZERS
OR DINNER. SELECT YOUR "SWEETS"
MENU PREFERENCES—EVERYONE
HAS A FAVORITE FLAVOR THAT
PAIRS WELL AFTER THE SAVORIES!

Strawberry Cupcakes

MAKES 24

1 cup butter, softened
¾ cup sugar
1 cup strawberry preserves
4 large eggs
3 cups all-purpose flour
1 teaspoon baking powder
1 teaspoon baking soda
½ teaspoon salt
1 (16-ounce) package frozen
sliced strawberries,
thawed and puréed
½ cup whole buttermilk
2 tablespoons strawberry
extract
Strawberry Filling
(recipe follows)
Fluffy Strawberry Frosting
(recipe follows)
Garnish: fresh strawberries

STRAWBERRY FILLING
MAKES ABOUT 3 CUPS

2 (16-ounce) containers frozen
sliced strawberries in syrup,
thawed and well drained
1 cup sugar
½ cup cornstarch
2 tablespoons fresh lemon juice
6 large egg yolks, lightly beaten
¼ cup butter, cubed
2 teaspoons strawberry extract

Preheat oven to 350°. Line 2 (12-cup) muffin pans with paper liners. In a large bowl, beat butter and sugar with a mixer at medium speed until creamy. Beat in strawberry preserves. Add eggs, one at a time, beating well after each addition.

In a medium bowl, whisk together flour, baking powder, baking soda, and salt. Gradually add flour mixture to butter mixture alternately with strawberry purée, beginning and ending with flour mixture, beating just until combined after each addition. Add buttermilk and strawberry extract, beating to combine. Spoon batter into prepared muffin cups, filling three-fourths full. Bake until a wooden pick inserted in center comes out clean, 18 to 20 minutes. Let cool in pans for 10 minutes. Remove from pans, and let cool completely on wire racks.

Using a melon baller, scoop out and discard about 1 tablespoon cake from center of each cupcake. Fill indentations with Strawberry Filling. Spread or pipe Fluffy Strawberry Frosting over cupcakes. Garnish with strawberries, if desired.

STRAWBERRY FILLING In the work bowl of a food processor or the container of a blender, purée strawberries until smooth.

In a medium heavy saucepan, combine sugar and cornstarch. Add strawberry purée, lemon juice, and egg yolks. Cook over medium heat, whisking constantly, until very thick, 7 to 8 minutes. Remove from heat; gradually whisk in butter until melted. Stir in strawberry extract. Let mixture cool slightly; cover and refrigerate for 2 hours.

FLUFFY STRAWBERRY FROSTING

Makes about 5 cups

**2 (8-ounce) packages cream
    cheese, softened**
½ cup butter, softened
2 cups confectioners' sugar
**1 (8-ounce) container frozen
    whipped topping, thawed**
2 tablespoons strawberry extract

In a large bowl, beat cream
cheese and butter with a mixer
at medium speed until creamy.
Gradually add confectioners' sugar,
beating until smooth. Add whipped
topping, beating to combine. Beat
in strawberry extract.

Recipe TIP

As visions of peppermints
dance through your head,
these meringues sit in the
oven overnight.

Peppermint Meringue Kisses

Preheat oven to 350°. Line 2 baking sheets with parchment paper.

In the work bowl of a food processor, place peppermint candies; pulse until finely chopped.

In the bowl of a stand mixer fitted with the whisk attachment, beat egg whites at high speed until foamy, about 1 minute. Add cream of tartar, and beat until fluffy but not dry. (Be careful not to overbeat.) Gradually add ⅓ cup sugar (about 3 tablespoons at a time), beating until combined. Beat in vanilla. Gradually add remaining ⅓ cup sugar, beating until mixture is glossy and sugar is dissolved, about 6 minutes. Gently fold in crushed peppermints.

Spoon meringue into a piping bag fitted with a round tip. Pipe meringue onto prepared pans in 1-inch circles, leaving a point at the top to make a "kiss" shape. Place pans in preheated oven, and turn oven off. Leave meringues in oven with door closed until crisp and dry, at least 2 hours or overnight.

MAKES ABOUT 24

1 cup peppermint candies
   (about 30 peppermints)
2 large egg whites, room
   temperature
½ teaspoon cream of tartar
⅔ cup superfine sugar,
   divided
1 teaspoon vanilla extract

Chocolate Tartlets

MAKES 12 SERVINGS

**3 (4-ounce) bars
  bittersweet
  chocolate, chopped**
**1 cup heavy whipping
  cream**
**1 (8.5-ounce) package
  prepared tart shells***
**Garnish: whipped
  topping, chocolate
  shavings, fresh mint
  leaves**

*We used Clearbrook Farms
Large Dessert-Size Sweet
Tart Ready-to-Fill Shells.*

In a medium bowl, combine chocolate and cream. Place bowl over a pan of simmering water, being careful not to touch the bowl to the water.

Cook, stirring frequently, until mixture is smooth. Spoon about 1½ tablespoons chocolate mixture into each prepared tart shell.

Refrigerate for 30 minutes. Once set, cover and refrigerate for up to 2 days. Garnish with whipped topping, chocolate shavings, and mint, if desired.

Recipe TIP

Melting chocolate with cream can also be done in the microwave on medium heat in 15-second intervals, stirring every 15 seconds, until fully melted.

Bear Claw Brownies

Preheat oven to 350°. Line a 13x9-inch baking pan with foil. Spray foil with baking spray with flour.

In a medium bowl, combine butter and chocolate. Microwave on high in 30-second intervals, stirring between each, until chocolate is melted and smooth (about 1½ minutes total).

In a large bowl, beat chocolate mixture and sugar with a mixer at medium speed until combined. Add eggs, one at a time, beating well after each addition. Add flour, vanilla, and salt, beating just until combined. Stir in cashews.

Spread batter into prepared pan. Drop caramel topping by teaspoonfuls over batter in pan. Using a knife, swirl caramel into brownie batter.

Bake until a wooden pick inserted in center comes out slightly sticky, 50 to 60 minutes. Let cool completely in pan.

MAKES 24

1½ cups butter
2 (4-ounce) bars 60% cacao bittersweet chocolate,* chopped
2 ½ cups sugar
4 large eggs
2 cups all-purpose flour
1 teaspoon vanilla extract
½ teaspoon salt
2 cups chopped cashews
1 (12-ounce) jar caramel topping*

*We used Ghirardelli Bittersweet Chocolate and Smucker's Hot Caramel Topping.

If you're short on time, use a boxed dark chocolate brownie mix and add cashews and caramel topping to make a quick and easy version of our Bear Claw Brownies.

Toasted Walnut Fudge

MAKES ABOUT 3½ POUNDS

3 cups sugar
½ cup butter
1 (5-ounce) can evaporated milk
1 (7-ounce) jar marshmallow crème
1 (12-ounce) package semisweet chocolate morsels
2 cups chopped toasted walnuts
1 teaspoon vanilla extract
¼ teaspoon salt

Line a 13x9-inch baking pan with foil. Spray foil with cooking spray.

In a Dutch oven, bring sugar, butter, and evaporated milk to boil over medium-high heat. Cook for 5 minutes, stirring constantly.

Remove from heat, and stir in marshmallow crème and chocolate morsels; stir just until melted and smooth. Stir in walnuts, vanilla, and salt.

Spoon mixture into prepared pan. Let stand until set, about 1 hour. Cut into 2-inch pieces.

Recipe TIP

The longer the custards
chill, the more easily the
caramel will release.

Crème Caramel

Preheat oven to 350°. Place 8 (6-ounce) ramekins in a roasting pan.

In a medium heavy saucepan, combine 3/4 cup sugar and 1/2 cup water. Cook over high heat until a candy thermometer registers 365° (sugar will be a medium amber color). Remove from heat, carefully swirling to distribute heat evenly. Carefully pour hot caramel into ramekins. Let stand until set, about 15 minutes.

In a medium bowl, whisk together eggs and egg yolks until combined.

In a medium saucepan, combine half-and-half, milk, cream, vanilla, salt, vanilla bean and reserved seeds, and remaining 3/4 cup sugar. Bring to a simmer over medium heat. Remove from heat. Whisk 1 cup hot cream mixture into egg mixture, whisking constantly. Pour hot egg mixture into remaining hot cream mixture, whisking constantly; strain mixture through a fine-mesh sieve into a bowl. Pour cream mixture over caramel in ramekins. Fill roasting pan with enough water to come halfway up sides of ramekins.

Bake until custards are set, about 1 hour. Let cool in roasting pan for 1 hour. Remove ramekins from pan; cover and refrigerate for at least 6 hours or up to 24 hours.

To unmold, gently run a sharp knife around edges of each ramekin, releasing custard and cutting into caramel at bottom. Invert ramekins onto plates, and gently jiggle to loosen. Serve immediately. Garnish with edible flowers, if desired.

MAKES 8 SERVINGS

1½ cups sugar, divided
½ cup water
4 large eggs
3 large egg yolks
1 cup half-and-half
½ cup whole milk
½ cup heavy whipping cream
2 teaspoons vanilla extract
¼ teaspoon salt
1 vanilla bean, split lengthwise, seeds scraped and reserved
Garnish: fresh edible flowers*

*Edible sugar flowers can be purchased at gourmetsweetbotanicals.com.

Salted Butterscotch Pots de Crème

1½ cups heavy
    whipping cream
1 cup half-and-half
½ cup firmly packed
    light brown sugar
2 tablespoons Scotch
1 teaspoon salt
1 teaspoon vanilla
    extract
½ teaspoon imitation
    butter flavoring
1 (12.25-ounce) jar
    butterscotch
    topping
8 large egg yolks
Garnish: sea salt

Preheat oven to 325°. Place a silicone baking mat in a large roasting pan. Place 8 (4-ounce) ovenproof demitasse cups or pot de crème cups on top of mat.

In a large saucepan, combine cream, half-and-half, brown sugar, Scotch, salt, vanilla, and butter flavoring over medium-high heat. Cook, whisking constantly, until mixture boils. Remove from heat. Add butterscotch topping, whisking to combine.

In a medium bowl, whisk together egg yolks. Using a ladle, pour 1 cup hot cream mixture into yolk mixture, whisking constantly.

Pour tempered egg mixture into cream mixture, whisking to combine. Return pan to heat, and cook over medium heat, stirring constantly, until mixture is thick enough to coat the back of a wooden spoon, or until mixture registers 170° on an instant-read thermometer. Remove from heat, and strain mixture through a fine-mesh sieve.

Divide mixture among serving cups. Fill roasting pan with enough water to come halfway up sides of cups. Cover pan with foil. Bake until set, about 1 hour and 15 minutes.

Remove roasting pan from oven; remove foil. Let cool in pan for 30 minutes. Remove pots de crème from pan; wrap each in plastic wrap. Refrigerate for at least 4 hours or overnight. Garnish with sea salt, if desired. Pots de crème will keep for up to 1 week wrapped tightly in plastic wrap.

Raspberry Clafoutis

Preheat oven to 350°. Spray 8 small ramekins or crème brûlée dishes with cooking spray.

In the bowl of a stand mixer fitted with the whisk attachment, beat milk, eggs, sugar, vanilla, and salt at medium speed until combined. Gradually add flour, beating until no lumps remain.

Arrange raspberries in a single layer in prepared dishes, and top each with batter.

Bake until center is set and top is lightly browned, about 30 minutes. Garnish with mint, if desired.

MAKES 8 SERVINGS

1½ cups milk
4 large eggs
½ cup sugar
1 tablespoon vanilla
   extract
⅛ teaspoon salt
¾ cup all-purpose flour
3 cups fresh raspberries
Garnish: fresh mint

Recipe TIP

This French dessert is traditionally made with fresh cherries; however, any soft and ripe fruit pairs well with the rich custard. Try it with blueberries, blackberries, strawberries, chopped peaches, or plums. Clafoutis batter can be refrigerated for up to 3 days. Simply whisk vigorously before pouring over fruit, and bake until lightly browned and set.

Lemon Cake with Raspberry Curd

Makes 1 (8-inch) cake

1 cup unsalted butter,
   softened
2 cups sugar
1 lemon, zested and juiced
4 large eggs
1 teaspoon vanilla extract
2¾ cups all-purpose flour
2½ teaspoons baking powder
½ teaspoon salt
1 cup whole milk
Raspberry Curd
   (recipe follows)
Lemon Buttercream
   (recipe follows)
Garnish: lemon slices,
   fresh raspberries

RASPBERRY CURD
Makes about 1½ cups

3 cups frozen raspberries*
½ cup sugar
1 lemon, zested and juiced
3 egg yolks
3 tablespoons cornstarch
⅛ teaspoon salt
4 tablespoons unsalted butter

*Frozen raspberries yield a
beautiful, bright red color. Fresh
raspberries are fine to use, but the
color will be a bit more muted.

Preheat oven to 350°. Spray 3 (8-inch) square cake pans with baking spray with flour. Line bottom of pans with parchment paper. In a large bowl, beat butter, sugar, and lemon zest and juice with a mixer at medium speed until fluffy, 3 to 4 minutes, stopping to scrape sides of bowl. Add eggs, one at a time, beating well after each addition. Beat in vanilla.

In a medium bowl, whisk together flour, baking powder, and salt. Gradually add flour mixture to butter mixture alternately with milk, beginning and ending with flour mixture, beating just until combined after each addition. Divide batter among prepared pans. Bake until a wooden pick inserted in center comes out clean, 20 to 25 minutes. Let cool in pans for 10 minutes. Remove from pans, and let cool completely on wire racks. Spread Raspberry Curd between layers. Spread Lemon Buttercream on top and sides of cake. Garnish with lemon slices and raspberries, if desired.

RASPBERRY CURD In a medium saucepan, combine raspberries, sugar, and lemon zest and juice over medium heat. Bring to a boil; reduce heat to medium-low, and simmer for 5 minutes. Transfer mixture to the container of a blender; process until smooth. Strain through a fine-mesh sieve; discard solids. Return mixture to saucepan, and increase heat to medium. In a medium bowl, whisk together egg yolks, cornstarch, and salt. Add about ¼ cup hot raspberry mixture to eggs, whisking constantly. Add egg mixture to remaining hot raspberry mixture. Cook over medium-high heat, whisking constantly, until thickened, 5 to 7 minutes. Remove from heat, and whisk in butter, 1 tablespoon at a time. Refrigerate for at least 2 hours.

LEMON BUTTERCREAM
MAKES ABOUT 4 CUPS

2 cups unsalted butter, softened
1 lemon, zested and juiced
4 cups confectioners' sugar

In a large bowl, beat butter with a mixer at medium-high speed until creamy. Add lemon zest and juice, beating until smooth. Gradually add confectioners' sugar, beating until combined after each addition.

Mini Almond-Praline Cakes

Preheat oven to 350°. Spray a 17x12-inch rimmed baking sheet with baking spray with flour. Line bottom of pan with parchment paper, and spray again.

In a medium bowl, beat cake mix, 1 cup water, almond paste, oil, eggs, and almond extract with a mixer at medium speed for 30 seconds. Increase mixer speed to high, and beat for 2 minutes. Spread mixture into prepared pan, smoothing top.

Bake until a wooden pick inserted in center comes out clean, about 15 minutes. Let cool completely.

Using a 3-inch round cutter, cut 20 rounds from cake, discarding scraps. Spread 2 to 3 tablespoons Praline Cream Filling over one cake round. Top with a second cake round, pressing down gently. Repeat with remaining cake rounds and filling. Place cakes on a wire rack set over a rimmed baking sheet.

In a medium microwave-safe bowl, combine candy coating and shortening. Microwave on high in 30-second intervals, stirring between each, until mixture is melted and smooth. Spoon mixture over cakes. Let stand until set, about 30 minutes. Cover and refrigerate for up to 3 days. Just before serving, garnish with edible sugar flowers, if desired.

PRALINE CREAM FILLING In a medium bowl, beat cream cheese with a mixer at medium-high speed until smooth. Add confectioners' sugar, almonds, and almond extract, beating to combine. Add whipped topping, and beat until smooth. Cover and refrigerate for up to 3 days.

MAKES 10 SERVINGS

1 (15.25-ounce) box classic white cake mix*
1 cup water
½ cup almond paste
⅓ cup vegetable oil
3 large eggs
1 teaspoon almond extract
Praline Cream Filling (recipe follows)
1 (16-ounce) package vanilla-flavored candy coating
3 tablespoons all-vegetable shortening
Garnish: edible sugar flowers**

*We used Duncan Hines Classic White Cake Mix.
**Edible sugar flowers can be purchased at gourmetsweetbotanicals.com.

PRALINE CREAM FILLING
MAKES ABOUT 3 CUPS

1 (3-ounce) package cream cheese, softened
¾ cup confectioners' sugar
¾ cup toasted sliced almonds, chopped
½ teaspoon almond extract
1 (12-ounce) container frozen whipped topping, thawed

Mini New York Cheesecakes

3 cups graham cracker crumbs
1 cup plus 6 tablespoons sugar, divided
¾ cup butter, melted
1 egg white, lightly beaten
2 (8-ounce) packages cream cheese, softened
½ cup sour cream
2 large eggs
2 tablespoons all-purpose flour
1½ teaspoons vanilla extract
Garnish: whipped cream, fresh strawberries, chocolate curls

Preheat oven to 350°.

In a small bowl, whisk together graham cracker crumbs, 6 tablespoons sugar, melted butter, and egg white. Press mixture into bottom and halfway up sides of 3 (12-cup) miniature cheesecake pans. Bake for 8 minutes.

In a large bowl, beat cream cheese and remaining 1 cup sugar with a mixer at medium speed until creamy. Add sour cream, eggs, flour, and vanilla, beating until smooth. Spoon about 1 tablespoon cream cheese mixture into each prepared crust.

Bake until set, 16 to 18 minutes. Let cool completely in pans. Cover and refrigerate before removing from pans. Garnish with whipped cream, strawberries, and chocolate curls, if desired.

Mini cheesecakes topped with strawberry slices or chocolate curls dance on a silver tray.

Beverages & Cocktails

SHARE THESE REFRESHING
DRINKS WITH GUESTS DURING
THE HOT SUMMERTIME OR WHEN
THE WEATHER IS CHILLY OUTSIDE.

Ginger Iced Tea

MAKES ABOUT 1 GALLON

2½ quarts cold water,
  divided
3 family-size tea bags
Ginger Syrup (recipe follows)
Garnish: cinnamon
  sticks, lemon curls

GINGER SYRUP
MAKES ABOUT 2½ CUPS

2 cups sugar
2 cups water
3 cinnamon sticks
2 tablespoons grated
  fresh ginger

In a medium saucepan, bring 1 quart cold water to a boil. Remove from heat, and add tea bags; cover and steep for 5 minutes. Strain tea into a large pitcher.

Add Ginger Syrup and remaining 1½ quarts cold water, stirring to combine. Serve over ice. Garnish with cinnamon sticks and lemon curls, if desired.

GINGER SYRUP In a medium saucepan, combine sugar and 2 cups water over medium-high heat, stirring until sugar is dissolved. Add cinnamon sticks and ginger.

Bring to a boil, reduce heat to medium-low, and simmer for 15 minutes. Cover and steep for 10 minutes. Strain mixture, discarding solids; let cool completely.

Warm Spice Orange Tea

MAKES ABOUT 2 QUARTS

7 cups water
1 (3-inch) piece ginger
8 whole cloves
4 cardamom pods
3 cinnamon sticks
2 star anise
2 family-size tea bags
1½ cups orange juice
½ cup honey
Garnish: quartered oranges
  slices, cinnamon stickers

In a Dutch oven, combine 7 cups water, ginger, cloves, cardamom, cinnamon sticks, and anise.

Bring to a boil; add tea bags. Reduce heat to low, and simmer for 5 minutes.

Remove tea bags. Stir in orange juice and honey, and simmer for 15 minutes. Strain mixture through a fine-mesh sieve into a serving pitcher to remove spices; serve hot.

Garnish with orange slices, and cinnamon sticks if desired.

WARM SPICE ORANGE TEA

Mango Green Tea Spritzers

Bring a small saucepan of water to a boil. Remove from heat, and add tea bags; cover and steep for 15 minutes.

Strain tea into a large container, and stir in sugar until dissolved. Add mango nectar and lemon juice, stirring to combine. Cover and refrigerate.

To serve, add sparkling water, and stir gently. Garnish with mango and mint, if desired.

MAKES 4 TO 6 SERVINGS

2 cups cold water
4 regular-size green
  tea bags
½ cup sugar
2 (11.3-ounce) cans
  mango nectar*
  (about 3 cups)
1 tablespoon fresh
  lemon juice
1½ cups sparkling water,
  chilled
Garnish: mango slices,
  fresh mint sprigs

We used Jumex Mango Nectar.

Every harvested tea begins as green tea, the oldest of all tea families. Green tea is widely sought after for its health benefits, and is in great demand in every tea-growing country.

Sparkling Lemonade

MAKES ABOUT 2½ QUARTS

2 cups superfine sugar
1 cup hot water
1½ cups fresh lemon
juice
1½ liters sparkling
seltzer water, chilled
Garnish: lemon slices

In a large pitcher, whisk together sugar and 1 cup hot water until sugar is dissolved.

Stir in lemon juice. Cover and refrigerate until cold, about 1 hour.

Just before serving, stir in sparkling water. Serve over ice. Garnish with lemon slices, if desired.

Pink Lemonade Punch

MAKES ABOUT 1 GALLON

1 (12-ounce) can frozen
pink lemonade
concentrate, thawed
1 (46-ounce) can pineapple
juice, chilled
2 tablespoons grenadine
1 (2-liter) bottle ginger ale,
chilled

In a large pitcher, combine pink lemonade concentrate, pineapple juice, and grenadine.

Add ginger ale, stirring gently to combine. Serve over ice.

SPARKLING LEMONADE

FESTIVE EGGNOG

Pumpkin Pie in a Mug

In a large saucepan, combine half-and-half, milk, and sugar over medium-low heat. Cook, stirring constantly, until sugar is dissolved.

Add pumpkin, vanilla, pumpkin pie spice, and salt, whisking to combine. Bring to a simmer, stirring occasionally; do not boil.

Garnish with whipped cream and pumpkin pie spice, if desired.

MAKES 6 SERVINGS

3 cups half-and-half
3 cups milk
3/4 cup sugar
1 cup canned pumpkin
2 tablespoons vanilla extract
2 teaspoons pumpkin pie spice
1/4 teaspoon salt
Garnish: whipped cream,
   pumpkin pie spice

Festive Eggnog

In a medium saucepan, combine milk, cinnamon, nutmeg, cloves, and vanilla. Cook over medium-low heat, stirring often, until milk begins to boil; remove from heat.

In a large bowl, beat yolks and brown sugar with a mixer at high speed until light and fluffy, about 5 minutes. Reduce mixer speed to medium-low; with mixer running, gradually add hot milk mixture to egg mixture. Pour mixture back into saucepan, and cook over medium heat, stirring constantly, until mixture thickens, 3 to 5 minutes. Be careful not to let mixture boil. Remove from heat; strain and discard solids.

Refrigerate for at least 4 hours. Stir in bourbon or rum. Whisk in whipped topping. Garnish with ground cinnamon, if desired. Serve immediately.

MAKES 6 SERVINGS

4 cups plain almond milk
1 teaspoon ground cinnamon
1/2 teaspoon freshly grated
   nutmeg
4 whole cloves
2 1/2 teaspoons vanilla extract
9 egg yolks
1 1/2 cups firmly packed light
   brown sugar
1 1/2 cups bourbon or rum
1 cup whipped topping
Garnish: ground cinnamon

Chai Eggnog Punch

Makes about 1 gallon

12 cups whole milk
1½ cups sugar
8 large eggs, lightly
  beaten
8 large egg yolks, lightly
  beaten
2 cups bourbon
2 tablespoons vanilla
  extract
1 teaspoon ground
  cinnamon
1 teaspoon ground
  nutmeg
1 teaspoon ground
  ginger
1 teaspoon ground
  cardamom
1 teaspoon ground
  cloves
½ teaspoon salt
Garnish: whipped cream,
  ground nutmeg

In a large Dutch oven, combine milk, sugar, eggs, and egg yolks over medium-low heat, whisking until smooth.

Cook, stirring constantly, until mixture coats the back of a spoon, 25 to 30 minutes. Remove from heat.

Strain milk mixture through a fine-mesh sieve into a large pitcher. Stir in bourbon, vanilla, cinnamon, nutmeg, ginger, cardamom, cloves, and salt.

Cover and refrigerate for at least 4 hours or up to 2 days.

Garnish with whipped cream and nutmeg, if desired.

Grapefruit and Basil Royale

In a cocktail shaker, combine ice, grapefruit juice, and Basil Simple Syrup. Cover and shake until cold. Strain into a chilled glass. Top with Prosecco.

Garnish with basil, grapefruit, and ginger, if desired.

BASIL SIMPLE SYRUP In a medium saucepan, bring sugar and 1 cup water to a boil over medium-high heat. Reduce heat to medium, and simmer until sugar is dissolved, about 10 minutes.

Remove from heat, and add basil. Let cool completely. Strain mixture through a fine-mesh sieve, discarding basil. Cover and refrigerate for up to 2 weeks.

MAKES 1 SERVING

1 cup ice
½ cup fresh-squeezed
    grapefruit juice
2 tablespoons Basil Simple
    Syrup (recipe follows)
½ cup Prosecco
Garnish: fresh basil,
    grapefruit slices,
    candied ginger

BASIL SIMPLE SYRUP
MAKES 1 CUP

1 cup sugar
1 cup water
1 cup fresh basil leaves

You may wish to assign someone to tend the bar so that you can spend more time with guests.

Thyme-Infused Pear Mimosas

MAKES 8 SERVINGS

4 cups pear nectar
1 (1-ounce) package
fresh thyme
2 teaspoons fresh
lemon juice
2 (750-ml) bottles
sparkling wine,*
chilled
Garnish: fresh thyme
sprigs

*To make nonalcoholic,
substitute 2 (750-ml)
bottles sparkling cider.

In a medium saucepan, bring pear nectar and thyme to a boil over medium-high heat. Reduce heat, and simmer for 10 minutes, stirring occasionally. Remove from heat and stir in lemon juice. Let cool completely.

Cover and refrigerate for at least 48 hours or up to 72 hours. Strain mixture through a fine-mesh sieve into a container; discard thyme.

For each serving, pour sparkling wine to fill half of a Champagne flute. Top with infused pear nectar. Garnish with thyme, if desired.

A perfect choice for a small luncheon
or shower to celebrate with cheer.

— *Recipe* TIP —

For a stronger rosemary flavor,
refrigerate the syrup overnight
before discarding rosemary sprigs.

Honey and Rosemary Champagne Cocktail

In a small saucepan, bring ¼ cup water, sugar, lemon juice, and rosemary to boil over medium heat.

Reduce heat, and simmer for 5 minutes. Remove from heat, and add whiskey. Let cool; discard rosemary.

Pour 1 tablespoon whiskey mixture into 8 (6-ounce) Champagne flutes; top with Champagne.

Garnish with lemon twists, if desired.

MAKES 8 SERVINGS

¼ cup water
¼ cup sugar
Juice of 1 lemon, plus
    peel for garnish
4 sprigs fresh rosemary
½ cup honey whiskey*
1 (750-ml) bottle
    Champagne

*We used Jack Daniel's Tennessee Honey.

Toasts are a great opportunity to welcome or congratulate guests. The host should offer the first toast—usually a well thought out one liner or a good joke, depending on what state you are from.

Mardi Gras Sangria

1 (750-ml) bottle red
    wine, such as
    Cabernet Sauvignon
1½ cups pineapple juice
1 cup orange juice
6 tablespoons Jamaican
    rum*
6 tablespoons brandy
Orange slices
Pineapple slices
Garnish: orange slices,
    pineapple slices

We used Appleton Jamaica Rum.

In a small pitcher, combine wine, pineapple juice, orange juice, rum, brandy, orange slices, and pineapple slices.

Refrigerate until chilled. Garnish with orange slices and pineapple slices, if desired.

Rather than preparing individual drinks for each party guest, offer a pitcher of Sangria. After you serve the first glass, guests can help themselves, and you will be free to mingle among friends.

White Russian

In a large pitcher, stir together eggnog, bourbon, rum, and hazelnut liqueur.

Garnish with star anise and cinnamon, if desired. Serve immediately.

MAKES 6 TO 8 SERVINGS

1 quart prepared eggnog
½ cup bourbon
½ cup dark rum
½ cup hazelnut liqueur*
Garnish: star anise,
   ground cinnamon

We used Frangelico.

The elegant Honey and Rosemary Champagne Cocktail on page 123, is simply suited for a celebration, while the creamy White Russian will warm you on a winter evening.

Coconut Daiquiris

Makes 4 servings

1 ripe banana
1 cup coconut rum
¾ cup cream of coconut
¾ cup light rum
2 tablespoons fresh
    lime juice
5 cups crushed ice

In the container of a blender, place banana, coconut rum, cream of coconut, light rum, and lime juice; process until combined.

Add ice; blend until smooth.

As refreshing as a breeze on a hot summer day, our sweet and creamy Coconut Daiquiris are frosty delights at any gathering.

Spicy Tequila Sunrise

In a cocktail shaker, combine ice, orange juice, and Pineapple-Jalapeño Tequila. Cover and shake until cold. Strain into 2 glasses filled with ice. Top each with 1 teaspoon grenadine. Garnish with lime and pineapple, if desired.

PINEAPPLE-JALAPEÑO TEQUILA Pour tequila into an airtight container. Add pineapple and jalapeño. Close container and shake. Refrigerate for 7 to 9 days, shaking once daily.

Using a slotted spoon, remove pineapple and jalapeño; discard. Line a funnel with two layers of cheesecloth, and slowly pour infused tequila through cheesecloth.

Line a funnel with a coffee filter. Pour tequila through funnel into an airtight container. Store in a cool, dry place.

MAKES 2 SERVINGS

2 cups ice
4 ounces orange juice
1 ounce Pineapple-Jalapeño
    Tequila (recipe follows)
2 teaspoons grenadine
Garnish: sliced lime,
    fresh pineapple

PINEAPPLE-JALAPEÑO TEQUILA

MAKES 1.75 LITERS

1 (1.75-liter) bottle silver
    tequila
1 fresh pineapple, peeled,
    cored, and diced
4 jalapeños, halved

Delight guests with garnishes that transport them to a beachside state of mind. Paper umbrellas and fresh fruit, though simple, it can also add a lot of appeal to already enticing beverages.

Bacon Manhattan

MAKES 2 SERVINGS

2 cups ice
1½ ounces Bacon Bourbon
(recipe follows)
¾ ounce sweet vermouth
¼ ounce blood orange
bitters
Garnish: Candied Bacon
Sticks (recipe follows)

BACON BOURBON
MAKES 1.75 LITERS

½ (16-ounce) package
thick-cut smoked
bacon
1 (1.75-liter) bottle
bourbon

CANDIED BACON STICKS
MAKES 4

4 slices thick-cut bacon
½ cup firmly packed
brown sugar
1 tablespoon chopped
walnuts (optional)

In a cocktail shaker, combine ice, Bacon Bourbon, vermouth, and bitters. Cover and shake until cold. Strain into 2 chilled glasses. Garnish with Candied Bacon Sticks, if desired.

BACON BOURBON In a large skillet, cook bacon over medium-high heat until almost burned. Remove bacon using a slotted spoon, reserving drippings in skillet.

Pour bourbon into an airtight container. Carefully pour hot bacon drippings into container. Close container and shake. Refrigerate for 7 to 9 days, shaking once daily. Remove from refrigerator, and freeze for 2 to 4 hours.

Spoon out hardened bacon fat, and discard. Line a funnel with two layers of cheesecloth, and slowly pour infused bourbon through cheesecloth. Repeat process, using another two layers of cheesecloth.

Line a funnel with a coffee filter. Pour bourbon through filter twice. Store in an airtight container in a cool, dry place.

CANDIED BACON STICKS Preheat oven to 375°. Line a rimmed baking sheet with foil. Spray foil with cooking spray.

Rub bacon with brown sugar, coating both sides. Place bacon in a single layer on prepared pan. Sprinkle with walnuts, if desired.

Bake until bacon is crisp, about 15 minutes. Remove from pans, and let cool completely on wire racks.

recipe index